Intelligence Is Not Enough

About the Author

Edward de Bono has been called 'the father of thinking about thinking'. He is the originator of the concept – and formal tools – of Lateral Thinking. He is regarded by many as the leading authority in the field of creative thinking, innovation and the direct teaching of thinking as a skill.

His methods are taught in thousands of schools around the world and his instruction in thinking has been sought by many business organisations over the years, including IBM, Prudential, Shell, Nokia, Bank of America and GM. He is on the Accenture list of the fifty most influential business thinkers in the world.

Dr de Bono was born in Malta. He was a Rhodes Scholar at Oxford, holds an M.A. in psychology and physiology from Oxford, a D. Phil. in Medicine, a Ph.D. from Cambridge, a D. Des. (Doctor of Design) from the Royal Melbourne Institute of Technology and an LL.D. from Dundee. He holds professorships at the Universities of Malta and Pretoria, Dublin City University and the University of Central England.

Intelligence Is Not Enough

Edward de Bono
(inventor of lateral thinking)

BLACKHALL
PUBLISHING

This book was typeset by Ark Imaging for

BLACKHALL PUBLISHING
33 Carysfort Avenue
Blackrock
Co. Dublin
Ireland
e-mail: info@blackhallpublishing.com
www.blackhallpublishing.com

© 2007 The McQuaig Group Inc
ISBN 978-1-84218-132-4
A catalogue record for this book is available from
the British Library.

All rights reserved. No part of this publication may be reproduced, stored in a retrieval system or transmitted in any form or by any means, electronic, mechanical, photocopying, recording or otherwise, without the prior, written permission of the publisher.

This book is sold subject to the condition that it shall not, by way of trade or otherwise, be lent, resold, hired out, or otherwise circulated without the publisher's prior consent in any form of binding or cover other than that in which it is published and without a similar condition including this condition being imposed on the subsequent purchaser.

Printed in the United Kingdom by Cromwell Press

INTRODUCTION

We use the word 'intelligence' to mean mental ability. So a highly intelligent person is much more mentally able than a person of lesser intelligence. We have also devised IQ tests so that we may measure just how intelligent a person may be.

This general use of the word 'intelligence' and IQ tests carry huge dangers.

You can test a person's eyesight and you may find that some people have extremely acute eyesight, much better than most other people. But if these 'superior eyesight' people are looking in the wrong direction that superior eyesight is of no value. A person with inferior eyesight who is looking in the right direction will be far more effective.

Intelligence is a potential. The way we use that potential is 'thinking skill'. Being intelligent does not mean that you have a high degree of thinking skill.

Intelligence is not enough and the belief that it is enough is dangerous.

SPEED

There is evidence to suggest that intelligence correlates well with the speed of transmission along the neurons in the brain. If the speed of transmission is high you can process things much faster. This means that all your mental activities are faster. So you can understand things more easily and recognise things more easily. You can scan through your memory bank more quickly. Mental operations of all sorts are carried out more quickly.

A young man is the son of a very rich property developer. For his twenty-first birthday his father gives him a Ferrari. The son has driven a bit before. He drives around in this powerful new car. He narrowly avoids some serious accidents.

INTELLIGENCE IS NOT ENOUGH

A young teacher saves on her salary to buy a car. She goes to driving school to learn how to drive. She takes a taxi occasionally to watch how the taxi driver copes in traffic. Eventually she buys a very small Fiat car. She drives slowly and carefully until she has build up her driving skill.

Now which is the better driver, the Ferrari driver or the Fiat driver?

There can be no doubt that the Ferrari is a much more powerful car than the Fiat. But does that make the Ferrari driver a better driver? There is no necessary relationship between the power of the car and the skill of the driver. The careful Fiat driver who has made an effort to learn how to drive may well be a better driver than the Ferrari driver.

It is the same with intelligence. Intelligence is the power and potential of the brain. The way that potential is used is equivalent to the driving skill. Thinking skill is equivalent to driving skill. In my experience many highly intelligent people are not good thinkers. At the same time, some less intelligent people are better thinkers.

The Intelligence Trap

Being tall is usually an advantage – especially when playing basketball. Being tall, however, means that you often hit your head on low doorways. Sometimes an advantage carries with it some disadvantages.

The intelligence trap is the trap into which highly intelligent people often fall.

Defence

A highly intelligent person can take up a position on a subject and then defend that position vigorously and ably with the full power of that superior intelligence. That intelligent person is able to dismiss the attacks of others less intelligent.

But the position taken up by the intelligent person may be based on limited past experience, prejudice or even emotions. The ability to defend this position ably and vigorously does not mean it is a valid position. By selecting evidence, values and perceptions it is possible to defend almost any position.

Instead of this vigorous defence of an initial position, a skilled thinker would have deliberately explored possible options and alternatives. The skilled thinker would have tried out different perceptions and would have made a serious effort to see the basis of other points of view.

Attack

Anyone who has grown up knowing that he or she is more intelligent than most people around would want to get the most satisfaction from his or her intelligence.

Our absurd habit of argument provides an excellent opportunity to display intelligence in attacking some other person's thinking. There is a triumph of ego and achievement. This is irresistible to intelligent people. You can show how intelligent you are – and how relatively stupid others might be. It is a primitive form of aggression carried out with less primitive means.

A more skilled thinker would not hasten to prove the other person wrong but would gently explore the subject to try to find out why the other person held a different view. That different view might be based on different experiences, different information, different values or different perceptions. It might also be based on prejudice or stupidity but that is for the thinker to discover, not to assume in the first place.

INTELLIGENCE TESTS

Intelligence tests had a valid and even noble origin. The intention was to identify those schoolchildren who were behind the average for their age group by reason of genetic or social impoverishment. The intention was that such children would benefit from special attention once they could be identified. For such purposes the intelligence tests were valid because they compared the performance of children with their peer group.

The difficulty arises at the other end when we seek to use IQ tests to identify very intelligent children. There is no comparison involved here except that some children do better at IQ tests than others.

IQ tests test the ability to do IQ tests. That is what they test.

If success at IQ tests correlates with success in some other field then the tests can be useful predictors of success in that field. If someone who does well at an IQ test also does well in accountancy exams then the test may indicate success in such exams. The test may also correlate with performance as an accountant.

The danger arises from the careless, sloppy and even dishonest use of the term 'intelligence'. This is a general use term meaning better at all mental activity and coping with life.

Suppose I designed a test which I chose to call a 'love test'. This consisted of the ability to distinguish between the scents of a number of roses. I would then suggest that those who did well at my 'love test' would be more loving parents. They would be better romantic partners. They would look after their pets better. Indeed, in any situation where love was involved they would outperform others. This would seem to be an outrageous claim – but it is not too far from the pretensions of IQ tests.

Research has shown that multiple-choice examinations mark down creative thinkers. The non-creative thinker finds the obvious answer quickly and gets the right mark. The creative thinker can consider the possibility of other answers – in special circumstances. That thinker may mark an answer that is then judged as 'wrong' because it is not usual. Even if the creative thinker does come back to the 'usual' answer, he or she will have spent much more time considering other possibilities. Exactly the same thing can happen with IQ tests when a creative thinker can see why an 'unusual' answer may be chosen.

Does this mean that Intelligence Tests are invalid? Not at all. They serve their original purpose very well. They also indicate the ability to do Intelligence Tests. We could reserve the term 'IQ-bility' for this and drop the general term 'intelligence'. Maybe they do test that speed of mind which we do want to call 'intelligence'. In that case we need to create a new word for 'coping with file' as intelligence no longer covers this meaning.

TEACHING THINKING

One afternoon Caroline Ferguson, one of my certified trainers, put together a workshop to generate ideas for a steel company in South Africa. Using just one of the formal tools of lateral thinking the group generated 21,000 ideas in an afternoon.

This particular tool was the 'random entry tool'.

Use of this tool is not 'intelligent behaviour'.

You take a completely random word and use it to generate ideas around a subject.

Since the word is random the same word could do for any conceivable subject. In the same way any word would do for any subject. This sounds like logical nonsense. But it is not.

In my book *The Mechanism of Mind* (1969) I describe how the nerve networks in the brain allow incoming information to arrange itself into patterns. All patterning systems are asymmetric and that is the basis of both humour and creativity. In the universe of such patterning systems the use of a random input is perfectly logical.

You live in a small town and whenever you leave your house you take the main road, which serves all your travel needs.

You do not bother with minor side roads. One day, your car breaks down on the outskirts of the town and you have to walk home. You ask for directions and find yourself arriving home by a road you had never taken on leaving home.

In exactly the same way, the random word drops you at the periphery of the subject and as you make your way to the centre of the subject you open up new possibilities that you had never thought of. The process is perfectly logical.

This is but one example of a 'deliberate tool for thinking'.

Software

You can have a very powerful computer with a huge processing speed. If, however, you do not have adequate software then that processing speed is not going to get you anywhere.

In exactly the same way high intelligence is the equivalent of fast processing speed. The tools and frameworks of thinking are the software needed for performance. Intelligence by itself is not enough.

Given the right software the intelligent person will use that software more powerfully than a less intelligent person. But intelligence itself is not a substitute for thinking software.

An intelligent person may understand the logic of the random word entry once it has been explained. Intelligence itself will not create that software.

Provocation

This is another process of lateral thinking. It is even more strange and different from normal logical thinking. It is also based on the behaviour of asymmetric patterning systems.

A factory by the side of a river puts out pollution which affects the people downstream. As a provocation we say:

'Po, the factory should be downstream of itself.'

(The word 'po' simply signals that what follows is a provocation. PO means 'provocative operation'.)

This statement seems illogical because how can the factory be downstream of itself?

With provocations we do not use our usual 'judgement' but we use a different mental operation called 'movement'. This operation involves ways of moving forward from a provocation to a new idea.

From the provocation we get the idea of legislating that if a factory is built on a river, its input must be downstream of its own output. In this way it is the first to get its own pollution. I have been told that this idea has become legislation in some countries.

'Po, taxi drivers do not know the way.'

This seems total nonsense since it contradicts the very notion of a taxi service. From the provocation comes the idea of a special type of taxi with a question mark on the roof. Such a taxi could only be used by residents who knew their way around their own town and could direct the driver. So, learner taxi drivers could be paid while they learned. That would provide more taxi drivers for everyone. In addition, residents would not be competing with tourists for taxis.

Wide Range

I have taught thinking to a very wide range of audiences:

From Down syndrome children to a class made up entirely of Nobel Prize winners.

From illiterate miners who had never been to school for even one day to top executives in corporations like IBM and DuPont.

From four-year-olds to ninety-year-olds – Roosevelt University in Chicago has a special programme for these seniors.

Thinking software (frameworks, tools, etc.) can be taught as a deliberate skill.

David Lane started to teach some of my thinking to very violent youngsters who had been sent to the Hungerford Guidance Centre in London because they were too violent to be taught at normal schools. In a twenty-year follow-up he showed that the actual rate of criminal conviction for those taught thinking was less than one-tenth the rate of those youngsters not taught thinking.

The simple point is that intelligence is not enough. Thinking needs to be taught as a deliberate skill.

THE GANG OF THREE

It would be absurd to claim that intelligent people do not already use some software, frame or thinking tools; of course they do.

But the software they use is what they have absorbed in education. That itself is the software in use in society – especially Western society.

Where did this software come from?

It came from the Greek Gang of Three (GG3) about 2,400 years ago. Since then we have done nothing about thinking – outside of mathematics.

Greek thinking came into Western Europe at the time of the Renaissance through the Arabs in Spain. At that time schools, universities and thinkers were all Church people. The sort of thinking they needed was truth, logic and argument to prove heretics wrong. This became the culture of thinking.

The Gang of Three were, of course, Socrates, Plato and Aristotle.

From Socrates came a love of dialectic and argument.

From Plato came the notion of ultimate truth.

From Aristotle came the 'box logic' we use today (something is judged to be in the box or outside – it could not be half in and half out and could not be anywhere else).

This judgement-based thinking has been so good that we have never thought to challenge or supplement it.

This thinking is indeed excellent just as the rear left wheel of a motor car is excellent. But it is not enough.

A doctor sees a child with a rash in his clinic. The doctor examines the child, takes the history and does some tests. When the doctor has 'judged' the condition to be measles the doctor immediately knows the probable course of the illness, the possible complications – and the treatment.

This is the model for almost all our thinking. You analyse the situation. You identify standard elements. Then you know how to response with standard action. This is the basis for one hundred per cent of education and ninety-five per cent of daily thinking.

Argument

From the GG3 comes our habit of argument. This is a primitive, crude and highly inefficient way of exploring a subject.

In a court of law if the prosecuting lawyer thinks of a point that will help the defence case will he bring up that point? Certainly not. And the other way around. The lawyers are not exploring the subject but making a case.

If the argument is a disagreement between possibility A and possibility B there is no effort to design C, D or E. There is no design energy.

If five per cent of the opposing case is wrong you spend all the time on that five per cent and not on the ninety-five per cent where there is agreement.

There is emotion and ego. There is attack and defence. There is winning and losing.

One day a man painted his car half black and half white. When his friends asked why he did this he explained that it was such fun to hear witnesses in court contradict each other whenever he had an accident. One witness would say a white car was involved but the other witness would maintain it was a black car. In any argument both sides may be right but they may be looking at a different part of the situation or different values.

For 2,400 years we have been happy with such an absurd system.

What else could we do?

We could have developed parallel thinking much earlier than 1985 when I first published my book on the Six Hats.

Four people are each facing one side of a building. Through a mobile phone each person is claiming that he or she is facing the most beautiful side of the building. With parallel thinking everyone moves round to one side. Then everyone moves round to another side – and so on. Everyone is now looking and thinking in parallel – not adversarially.

Six Hats

I was told by a Nobel Prize-winning economist that he found the Six Hats method in use at a top economics meeting in the USA. A woman told me how she had been teaching the Six Hats in an almost Stone Age culture and how they said it had changed the people's lives. The method is in use with four-year-olds in schools and with top executives.

The method reduces thinking time to one-quarter or even one-tenth of what it usually was. A corporation in Finland reported that meetings that had taken thirty days in the past were now completed in two days. In the USA Grant Todd pioneered the use of the system with juries in court and showed that they reached unanimous decisions very quickly.

The Hats are used as a symbol to indicate a particular mode of thinking. When a particular colour of hat is in use then everyone thinking, in parallel, in that mode.

White Hat: focus on information. What information is available? What information is missing? Questions: how do we get the information we need?

Red Hat: permission to put forward your feelings, emotions and intuition without any need to explain or justify them.

Black Hat: caution, careful. The downside. Why something is wrong or may not work. Critical and outlines how something does not fit our ethics, our budget, etc.

Yellow Hat: focus on the benefits and values. The positive aspects and ways of doing something.

Green Hat: creativity. New ideas and possibilities. Modifications of the idea. The formal use of lateral thinking tools.

Blue Hat: the organising hat which decides the focus and the desired outcome of the thinking. This hat also keeps discipline and decides the order in which the hats are to be used. Also puts together the outcome of the meeting.

I have hundreds of trainers in different countries around the world who are certified to train the method.

Different Software

Just by being intelligent an intelligent person does not automatically get access to this new software. So that person is trapped in the use of the judgement-based software of the Greek Gang of Three.

PERCEPTION

Gödel's famous theorem shows how from within any system you can never logically prove the starting points. So no matter how logical you might be, you can never do better than your starting points, which are arbitrary perceptions and arbitrary values. These are determined by culture, experience and even the mood of the moment.

While our thinking culture has put huge emphasis on logic we have done almost nothing about perception (probably for religious reasons). David Perkins at Harvard has shown how ninety per cent of the errors in thinking are errors of perception and not of logic at all.

This is important because the intelligent person tends to pride him or herself on logical ability. Such ability is worse than useless if perceptual skills are not developed. It is worse than useless because impeccable logic leads to a feeling of certainty and arrogance that is not open to change.

Perceptual Tools

Can we do anything about perception? The perceptual tools that I designed are part of the CoRT (Cognitive Research Trust) programme, which is now used in thousands of schools around the world. This programme contains simple tools for direction attention.

Thirty boys aged around twelve years old were asked if it would be a good idea for students to be paid for attending school. All thirty decided it would be a good thing. They then applied the very simple perceptual tool of the PMI (Plus, Minus and Interesting), which asks the thinker to direct attention to the Plus points, the Minus points and the Interesting points. At the end of this brief exercise twenty-nine of the boys had changed their minds and decided it was not a good idea.

Two hundred and fifty top women executives in Canada were asked if women should be paid more than men for doing the same job. Eighty-six per cent thought it a good idea. They were then asked to do a C&S (Consequence & Sequel), which directs attention to immediate, short-term, medium-term and long-term consequences. The number in favour dropped to just fifteen per cent. Yet every one of those top executives would have claimed that she spent her life looking at consequences in her executive role.

In the Karee mine in South Africa there used to be two hundred and ten fights a month between the seven tribes working there. These fights were based on traditional enmities. The CoRT attention-directing tools were taught to these miners by Donalda Dawson and Susan Mackie. The OPV (Other People's View) tool requires the thinker to get inside the mind of the other party. The fights dropped to just four a month.

The tools are so unbelievably simple that many educators believe they cannot work. But they work very well. The tools are given acronyms so that they have a location in the brain. Attitudes have no location.

An intelligent person would claim that he or she did not need such simple tools because any intelligent person would behave this way anyway. Unfortunately, this is not true at all and is typical of the arrogant claims made for intelligence.

Changing Perception

In Australia a five-year-old boy called Johnny was offered a choice of coins by his friends. There was a two-dollar coin and a one-dollar coin. His friends told him he could choose and keep whichever one he wanted: he chose the one-dollar coin, which is much bigger than the two-dollar coin. His friends laughed at him. Whenever they wanted to tease him they offered him the same coins. He always took the larger one.

One day an adult saw this and beckoned Johnny over. He told Johnny that the smaller coin, even though smaller, was actually worth twice as much as the bigger coin. Johnny nodded politely and said that he knew that: 'but how often would they have offered him the coins if he had taken the two dollars the first time?'

If Johnny had perceived the situation as a one-off matter he would have chosen the bigger value. But he knew his friends and saw it as a longer-term matter.

Changing perception is not a matter of intelligence but of the willingness to explore possibilities.

Universities

A few months ago I was in Bangkok giving a talk at the World University Presidents' Summit. There were hundreds of university presidents from all around the world.

The point I was making was that universities are somewhat out of date. The original purpose of a university was to collect the wisdom of the ages and make it available to the youngsters of today. Because of the excellence of the digital age we can now get any information we want when we want it. There is no need for a university as a source of knowledge.

Universities should be involved in teaching skills: thinking skills, people skills, management skills, etc.

When I used to examine in the medical final examinations at Cambridge University I asked the students where they got their knowledge. They said that they went to hospital to prod a few patients and this was motivational. You would never see enough cases to give you the information you needed. They went to lectures to find out the level of information they were required to have. They did all their real studying from books.

Universities are all about 'what is'. This is knowledge, information and descriptions of things. Such knowledge and understanding is important and even essential. Knowing your way around the world and around your chosen subject is necessary.

Equally important, however, is dealing with 'what can be'. This is to do with how you bring things about. Traditionally universities have not been good at that. They may teach the skill of presenting information but that falls far short of the thinking involved in making things happen.

I am often chided for not having lists of references at the back of my books. I tell those who complain that this is because my books are my ideas and are not culled from a review of the literature. I am in the business of designing tools and software for human thinking – not reviewing what others may have felt about thinking. I am a designer not a historian. Sadly, the academic mindset finds this difficult to deal with.

There is some evidence that universities may be changing but it is a very slow process because there is so much defence of the status quo.

DESIGN

Western thinking culture and universities have been all about analysis. We have never given 'design' an equal ranking with analysis. Yet the future is going to depend on design.

We have thought it enough to leave design to talented individuals whose thinking has not been crippled by their university careers.

Things are beginning to change and in the USA universities and colleges are opening 'design centres'. This is a bit late and about forty years after I first emphasised the importance of design.

The emphasis is on the freedom of creativity and the value of cross-disciplinary teams. These are useful but are very weak approaches to the subject of design.

The motivation seems to be that China is taking over manufacture because the wage rate in China is very low. A production worker makes about one hundred dollars a month. In India the wages may be even lower at fifty dollars a month – compared to one or two thousand dollars a month in the West.

So the idea is that the East will take on the 'grunt work' and the West will survive on innovation and creativity. Unfortunately, this leaves out the consideration that China and the East may actually learn the skills of creativity and design ahead of the West. This is because the West has a very old-fashioned view of creativity and design and the Chinese are more eager to learn the formal skills of creativity and design. I have been invited to China and India many times to give seminars and the government is doing a pilot project with my work in schools. There is more openness and less defensiveness.

There is a new programme that I have developed to teach design thinking. It is called Design and may be used in colleges and universities.

Design is the ability to deliver value from the ingredients at hand.

How does this relate to intelligence? Because intelligent people understand and play the game in which they are placed. So they become excellent at understanding and analysis but never develop the skills of design.

Intelligence is usually concerned with the truth. Design is concerned with possibility and value.

You can have truth about the past but you can only have possible value about the future.

Creativity

Highly creative people do not usually regard themselves as creative. Creativity seems to be a different game based on chance, inspiration and uncertainty. An intelligent person likes to have everything under his or her control. An intelligent person likes to proceed logically, step by step, through analysis and deduction to arrive at a proven conclusion. The notion of sitting by a stream, playing Baroque music and hoping for some new idea is not very attractive to highly intelligent people who like to have things under their control instead of waiting for the inspiration of a new idea.

The above view is understandable given the old-fashioned view of creativity. All that has now changed.

Society has always regarded creativity as an aberration, as an exception and as some mysterious gift possessed only by a few people. Society has been so unwilling to deal with creativity that we do not even have a word (at least not in the English language) to distinguish between artistic creativity and idea creativity. That is one of the reasons it was necessary to create the term 'lateral thinking', which I did in 1967.

As soon as I claim that creativity is a mental skill that can be learned, practiced and developed, people ask if I could train a new Beethoven. I make no such claim for artistic creativity, which is an amalgam of many aptitudes, but I do make the claim for idea creativity.

Logical Basis for Idea Creativity

Once we start looking at the brain as a self-organising neural network we can understand the logical basis for creativity (see my book *The Mechanism of Mind*, 1969). Such systems form patterns. Patterning systems are always asymmetric (the route from A to B is rarely the same as the route from B to A).

Lateral thinking implies moving 'sideways' across patterns to go from the main pattern to a side pattern. Once there we can easily see the route back to the starting point.

All valuable creative ideas will always be logical in hindsight. It is then claimed that if the idea is logical in hindsight it should be accessible by logic in the first place – so there is no need for creativity. This is total rubbish and arises because philosophers and psychologists have been playing with words and have not seen the behaviour of asymmetric patterning systems.

The trunk of a tree divides into two. Each part then splits into two branches – and so on. What are the chances of an ant on the trunk of the tree reaching a specified leaf. At every branch point the chances diminish by one over the number of new branches. In an average tree the chances would be about one in eight thousand. Now imagine the ant on the specified leaf – what are the chances of that ant reaching the trunk of the tree? The chances are one in one or a hundred per cent. There are no forward branches so the ant just moves forward and will certainly reach the trunk of the tree. This is how asymmetric systems work.

The Tools

Once we have understood the logical basis for creativity we can then design specific thinking tools that will enable us to generate ideas in a formal and deliberate manner, instead of waiting for ideas by the river.

The tools include challenge, concept extraction, concept fan, provocation, and movement and random entry.

All the tools can be learned and used deliberately. With practice, skill in the use of the tools increases. For example, the mental operation of 'movement' needs to be developed otherwise we are restricted to judgement. Movement is not just an absence of judgement, as in brainstorming, but a deliberate mental operation.

Intelligence and Creativity

At this point intelligent people can now decide that they can be creative if they want to. More than that, their superior speed of mental processing means that they will probably use the tools more effectively than others.

But they have to want to learn and try to be creative. It will not just happen to them because of their intelligence.

Operacy

Education has always been about literacy and numeracy. This is because education has never been able to shake off its historic baggage.

Many centuries ago most people did not know how to read and write. Reading, writing and number work were done by the 'scribes'. Everyone else got on with the daily business of living and working. So education was intended for these scribes. When education was opened to everyone it still kept a curriculum, and mission, based on educating the scribes.

The equivalent of scribes will soon emerge in today's society. These will be 'information masters' and their profession will be to access the Internet and other information sources to prepare information packages for their clients.

The education designed for the scribes definitely did not contain operacy because this is exactly what the scribes would not be doing. Operacy is a word I invented to cover the 'skills of doing'.

Youngsters may learn literacy and numeracy at school but as soon as they leave school they are going to have to 'operate' in the real world of action. This requires operacy.

It is supposed that operacy will be acquired through a period of apprenticeship and learning on the job. Specific skills may be learned that way but the general skills of operacy are best learned at school.

For several years I was Chairman of Young Enterprise Europe. We had one and a half million youngsters in Europe, Russia and Israel who set up mini-businesses while still at school. One year the top prize was won by a team of twelve-year-old boys who designed a 'one stop' wedding site on the Internet. You could order the hall, the music, the food and everything (except the bride) at one place.

This was one approach to operacy — there are many others.

Analysis is not enough.

Analysis leads to understanding. Understanding does not necessarily lead to action unless there is a routine response to a routine situation.

Intelligent people are excellent at analysis and understanding but not so good at designing and carrying out action. This may be because they are more comfortable with analysis. This may be because their intelligence allows them to see more risks than others in action and they do not want to take these risks.

The term 'analysis paralysis' is an exaggeration but indicates a preference for analysis over action.

Thinking and Action

The famous French philosopher René Descartes is best known for his saying:

'Cogito ergo sum'.

This means: 'I think therefore I am'.

This, together with Rodin's awful sculpture of the solemn thinker, gives the idea that thinking is all about thinking.

So it was necessary to design a new quote:

'Ago ergo erigo'.

This means: 'I act therefore I build'.

Thinking is not just about contemplation and playing elaborate philosophical word games but also about action – about making things happen.

It is not enough to be intelligent; there is a need for intelligence to be put to work in action.

ARROGANCE

I have worked with Down syndrome children and with totally illiterate miners in Africa. They may not be well-informed but they are not stupid. They can also be taught thinking.

In my experience there is only one form of stupidity and that is arrogance.

Arrogance is a communication sin. Arrogance means cutting all lines of inward communication from the world around. The outward communication continues but there is a complete lack of sensitivity to inward communication. So there is no change and no learning.

Highly intelligent people can have a fully justified sense of arrogance. They are superior and they know it. Unfortunately, arrogance – no matter how justified – always carries with it the dangers of arrogance.

Highly intelligent people sometimes give the impression that they know it all and there is nothing that they need to learn. This applies in particular to anything to do with mental activity. They are proud and complacent about their thinking ability, which is indeed excellent in analysis but not developed in other areas.

This attitude leads to a huge waste of that superior mental processing. Applied to new thinking tools and frameworks that processing can be very powerful. Sitting in a swamp of complacency, intelligence is not enough.

Intelligence demands the intelligent use of intelligence.